The Nature Kid's Guide to
MANATEES

DAVID ANDERSON

For information address LP Media Inc. Publishing,
30012 Variolite St NW, Princeton MN 55371
www.lpmedia.org

Publication Data

Manatees
The Nature Kid's Guide to Manatees — First edition.

Summary: "Learn all about Manatees, the Nature Kid Way"
— Provided by publisher.

ISBN: 979-8-89818-148-2

[1. Manatees – Non-Fiction] I. Title.

Title: The Nature Kid's Guide to Manatees

CONTENTS

WARM WATERS
DID YOU KNOW?
Manatees are close relatives of elephants! You can see the connection in their thick, wrinkly skin and toenail-like flippers.

Glide! A big manatee floats down a warm, sunny river.

Manatees love warm water. They live in rivers, bays, and shallow seas. If the water drops below 68 degrees, they search for warmer spots right away.

These gentle animals are sometimes called sea cows. They float near the top of the water, coming up to breathe before sinking back down. Their slow, peaceful movements make them fun to watch.

Some manatees swim near warm springs in winter. The springs keep their big bodies cozy. It is like a warm bath all day long!

MAP MATES

FUN
FACT!
Some Florida manatees travel
over 500 miles each year just to
find warm water!

Whoosh! A manatee swims through a wide jungle river.

Three kinds of manatees live around the world. West Indian manatees swim near Florida and the Caribbean. They like bays, rivers, and coasts.

Amazonian manatees live in rivers deep in South America. They stay in fresh water their whole lives and never swim in the ocean. These are the smallest manatees of all.

West African manatees live along the coast of Africa. Each kind has its own special home, but all three share some amazing things in common — and you are about to learn them all!

MEGA MAMMALS

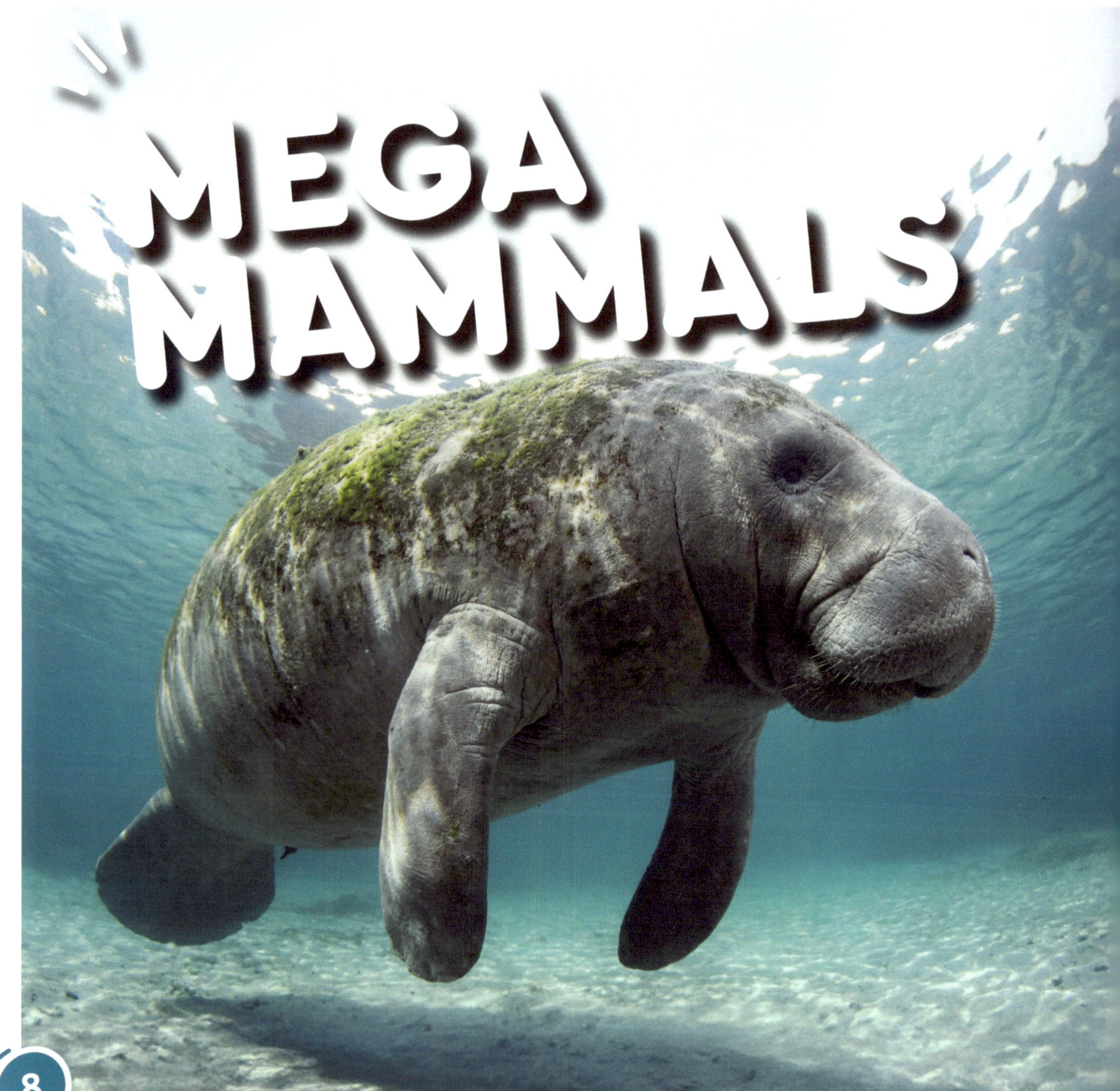

Thump! A huge manatee swims down a shallow sandy shoreline.

A grown manatee can be ten feet long and weigh about 1,000 pounds. Some big ones tip the scales at 1,200 pounds or more. That is heavier than a grand piano!

Even though they are so big, manatees are round and soft. Their plump body shape helps them float easily. They look like giant gray logs drifting in the water.

A manatee can live for more than 65 years. One famous Florida manatee named Snooty lived to be 69!

FLIPPER FUN

DID YOU KNOW?

Manatee teeth wear down from chewing tough plants, but when the old ones wear out new teeth will grow in from the back.

Swish! A manatee waves its flat tail and glides forward.

Two small flippers stick out from each side, and a wide, flat tail pushes from behind. Together they make a surprisingly graceful swimmer for such a big animal!

Each flipper has three or four small nails at the tip. These look like tiny toenails! Manatees use their flippers to steer, crawl along the bottom, and scoop food toward their mouths.

The flat tail moves up and down, not side to side like a fish tail. One strong push sends the manatee gliding through the water.

SUPER SNOUTS

Manatees have special hairs all over their body that sense movement—it's like having thousands of tiny fingertips!

Sniff! A manatee pokes its big nose above the water.

A manatee's snout is covered in thick whiskers. About 600 of them! These whiskers help it feel things in the water. Even in dark, cloudy water, a manatee can find food.

Manatees have small eyes, but they can see pretty well. They can even see colors! Their ears are tiny holes on the sides of their head, almost hidden in their skin.

A manatee's upper lip can move and flex on its own, almost like a tiny trunk. It reaches out, grips a plant, and pulls it straight into the mouth!

TOUGH SKIN

A manatee's skin can be almost two inches thick in some spots—that is thicker than a stack of ten pennies!

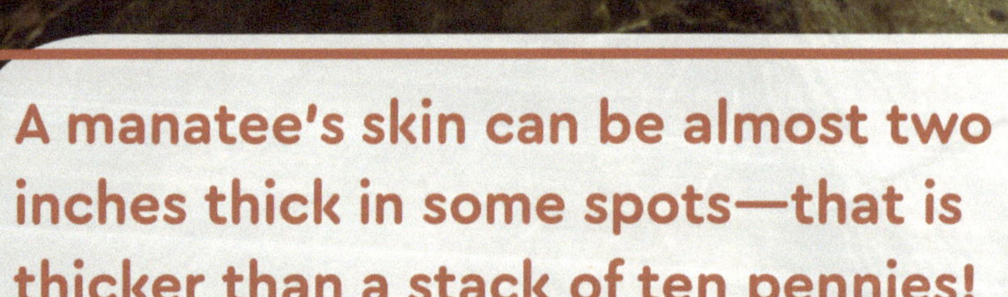

Scrape! A manatee rubs its thick skin on a rough log.

Manatees have very thick, tough skin. It is gray and wrinkly, almost like an elephant's, and does a good job protecting them from scrapes and bumps along rocky riverbeds and boat hulls.

Sometimes tiny plants called **algae** grow right on their skin. This can turn a manatee slightly green! Small fish will swim up and nibble the algae clean off, giving the manatee a free spa treatment!

Manatees have almost no fur, which is unusual for a **mammal**. But their skin is tough enough to do the job all on its own.

GRASS GRAZERS

Munch! A manatee chomps on a big bunch of seagrass.

Manatees are **herbivores**. That means they eat only plants. They munch on **seagrass**, water weeds, and other water plants all day long.

A manatee spends six to eight hours eating every day. It uses its big, split upper lip to grab food. The two sides move like hands pulling in plants.

Seagrass grows on the sandy bottom of rivers and bays. Manatees swim along the bottom and graze like cows in a field. No wonder people call them sea cows!

A manatee can eat over 100 pounds of plants in a single day.

SQUEAK SPEAK

Squeak! A young manatee calls out to its mama nearby.

Manatees talk to each other with squeaks, chirps, and squeals. These sounds travel well under the water and help manatees stay close in a group.

When manatees are scared or excited, they make louder sounds. Happy manatees may squeak softly while they eat. Mothers and calves call back and forth to find each other.

Most of their sounds are too quiet for people to hear from above. But if you listen under the water, you can hear them chatting away!

FRESH AIR

Long ago, sailors thought manatees were mermaids. Maybe the sailors needed glasses!

Poof! A manatee pops its nose above the water and takes a big breath.

Even though manatees live underwater, they breathe air just like you do. Two nostrils sit on top of their snout. When a manatee dives, special flaps snap shut to keep water out. When it surfaces, they pop open for a breath.

A manatee can hold its breath for up to 20 minutes when resting. When swimming around, it needs air every three to four minutes.

The most amazing part is that sleeping manatees breathe without waking up. Their body just knows when to rise, take a breath, and sink back down. It happens all night long!

CURIOUS GIANTS

Boop! A manatee swims right up and bumps a diver's hand.

Manatees are not just gentle — they are genuinely curious. They will often swim toward something new just to check it out. Divers in Florida are regularly visited by manatees who nudge their flippers and investigate their gear!

This curiosity means manatees are also surprisingly smart. Scientists have trained them to touch different shapes and colors to earn food, and they pick it up fast.

Most wild animals run from the unknown. Manatees swim straight toward it. For an animal that moves so slowly, that kind of boldness is pretty remarkable!

SLOW SWIM

DID YOU KNOW?
A scared manatee can swim up to 15 miles per hour—that is three times faster than an Olympic swimmer!

Glub! A manatee drifts by as slow as a floating cloud.

Most of the time, manatees swim very slowly. They drift along at about three to five miles per hour. That is slower than most people walk!

Manatees do not need to go fast. They are not chasing food. Plants do not run away! So there is no rush at all.

But if a manatee gets scared, it can speed up fast. One big push of the tail sends it zooming away. They save this burst of energy for when they really need it.

LAZY DAYS
DID YOU KNOW?
Manatees control whether they
sink or float by moving gas
through their stomach!

Bubble! A resting manatee lets out a puff of air below.

Manatees like to take it easy. They sleep, rest, and drift for much of the day. When they nap, they sink to the bottom and pop up to breathe.

A sleeping manatee comes to the top about every three to five minutes for a breath. Then it sinks back down to rest some more. Some manatees even sleep floating upright underwater, hovering like a giant slow-motion balloon!

When awake, manatees look for food or just paddle around. Some like to roll, scratch on rocks, and play near the surface. Life is slow and peaceful for a manatee.

Sometimes more than 300 manatees gather at one warm spring in Florida. It looks like a manatee party!

Bump! Two manatees touch noses and greet each other.

Manatees are sometimes alone, but not always. They often come together in small herds. Other times, they swim on their own for days.

When manatees meet, they often touch noses and bodies. This gentle rubbing is their way of saying hello. They may swim together for a while before drifting apart.

Groups can form at feeding spots or warm resting areas. These meetups are calm and quiet. Manatees seem to enjoy just hanging out together.

MAKING
MATES

Splish! A female manatee quickly swims away from several males!

When it is time to mate, male manatees follow a female. Sometimes many males swim after one female at once. This group is called a mating herd.

The males push and bump to get close to her. They may follow her for days or even weeks! It looks like a slow parade through the water.

After mating, the male swims away. The female will carry the baby inside her for about 12 months before it is born.

A mating herd can include up to 20 males chasing one female for weeks!

CUTE CALVES

A manatee calf nurses from a spot right behind its mother's flipper—like a secret milk station!

Swoosh! A newborn calf pops up for its very first breath.

Baby manatees are called calves. They are born under the water! The mother quickly pushes the calf to the top for its first breath of air.

A newborn calf weighs about 60 pounds and is about 4 feet long. That is about the size of a big dog. It can swim from the start, but it stays close to its mother.

Calves drink milk from their mother for the first year or two. They start to munch on plants after just a few weeks, learning by watching mom.

MAMA MOVES

A mother manatee has only one calf at a time. Twins are super rare.

Whomp! A mama manatee softly pushes her calf to the surface.

Mother manatees take great care of their calves. A calf stays with its mother for one to two years. She teaches it where to find food and warm water.

The mother and calf swim side by side, almost touching. The calf often rests on its mother's back. She keeps it safe and close at all times.

Mama manatees are very patient. They let their calves play and explore, but always keep watch. A mother's love keeps the calf safe until it is ready to live on its own.

BOAT
DANGER

DID YOU KNOW?
Scientists can tell manatees apart by their scars. Each manatee has a unique pattern, like a fingerprint!

Vroom! A manatee hears a boat engine and swims away.

Boats are the biggest danger to manatees. These animals rest near the top of the water, right where boats zoom by. Fast boats can hit them before they can move out of the way.

Many manatees have scars on their backs from boat **propellers**. Some are hurt very badly. Almost every wild manatee in Florida has at least one scar.

Losing **habitat** is also a problem. When clean water and seagrass disappear, manatees have less food and fewer safe places to live. They need our help.

SAFE SPOTS

Every November, Florida celebrates Manatee Awareness Month. Some towns even have manatee parades!

Click! A scientist takes a photo of a manatee and smiles.

People are working hard to keep manatees safe. In Florida, there are special zones where boats must go slow. Signs warn boaters to watch for manatees below.

Protected areas guard the warm springs where manatees gather. These spots give manatees room to rest, eat, and raise their young without being disturbed.

Thanks to these efforts, manatee numbers have grown from about 1,000 in the 1970s to over 7,500 today. There is still more work to do, but the future looks brighter for these gentle giants.

GLOSSARY

herbivore

An animal that eats only plants

mammal

A warm-blooded animal that feeds milk to its babies

algae

Tiny plant-like living things that grow in water or on wet surfaces

seagrass

A plant that grows underwater in shallow, sunny parts of the ocean

habitat

The place where an animal lives in the wild

propeller

The spinning metal blades on a boat engine

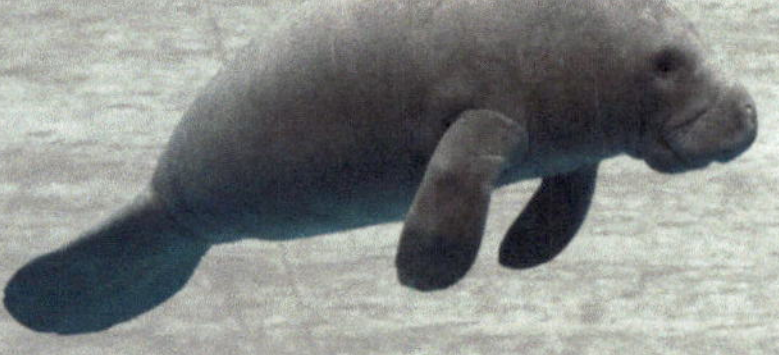